Itty Bitty Babies™

General Information

Many of the products used in this pattern book can be purchased from local craft, fabric and variety stores, or from the Annie's Attic Needlecraft Catalog (see Customer Service information on page 27).

Boy's Summer Sweater

SKILL LEVEL

INTERMEDIATE

FINISHED SIZE

Fits 5-inch baby doll

MATERIALS

- Size 10 crochet cotton:
  100 yds each cream and blue
- Size 6/1.80mm steel crochet hook or size needed to obtain gauge
- Tapestry needle
- Sewing needle
- Blue sewing thread
- Tiny button

GAUGE

9 sc = 1 inch; 8 sc rows = 1 inch
15 hdc = 2 inches; 7 hdc rows = 1 inch

PATTERN NOTES

Chain-2 at beginning of row or round does not count as first half double crochet unless otherwise stated.

Join with slip stitch as indicated unless otherwise stated.

INSTRUCTIONS

SWEATER

Row 1: Beg at neck edge, with blue, ch 29, 2 sc in 2nd ch from hook and in each ch across, turn. *(56 sc)*

Row 2 (RS): Ch 1, sc in each of first 8 sts, ch 7, sk next 12 sts *(armhole)*, sc in each of next 16 sts, ch 7, sk next 12 sts *(armhole)*, sc in each of last 8 sts, turn. *(32 sc)*

Row 3: Ch 1, sc in each st and in each ch across, turn. *(46 sc)*

Rows 4–8: Ch 1, sc in each st across, turn. At end of last row, **do not turn**.

Rnd 9: Now working in rnds, 2 sc in same st as last sc, working in ends of rows, evenly sp 5 sc across to end of row 2, sc in end of row 2, ch 3 *(button loop)*, sc in end of row 1, working in starting ch on opposite side of row 1, 2 sc in first ch, sc in each ch across, with 2 sc in last ch, evenly sp 6 sc across to first sc of row 8, 2 sc in same st as first sc, **join** *(see Pattern Notes)* in first sc of row 8. Fasten off.

SLEEVES

Rnd 1: Join blue with sc in center ch of ch-7 of armhole, sc in each of next 3 chs, **sc dec** *(see Stitch Guide)* in end of next row and first sk st, sc in each of next 10 sk sts, sc dec in next sk st and end of next row, sc in each of last 3 chs, join in beg sc. *(19 sc)*

Rnds 2–6: Ch 1, sc in each st around, join in beg sc. At end of last rnd, fasten off.

Rep on rem armhole.

Sew button opposite button loop.

SHORTS

Rnd 1: With cream, ch 36, being careful not to twist ch, sl st in first ch to form ring, **ch 2** *(see Pattern Notes)*, hdc in first ch and in each ch around, join in beg hdc. *(36 hdc)*

Rnds 2–7: Ch 2, hdc in first st and in each st around, join in beg hdc.

FIRST LEG

Rnd 1: Ch 3, sk first 18 hdc, sl st in next hdc, ch 2, hdc in same st and in each of next 17 sts, hdc in each of next 3 chs, join in beg hdc. *(21 hdc)*

Rnds 2 & 3: Ch 2, hdc in first st and in each st around, join in beg hdc. At end of last rnd, fasten off.

2ND LEG

Rnd 1: With RS facing, join in first hdc of rnd 7, ch 2, hdc in same st and in each of next 17 sts, hdc in each of next 3 chs, join in beg hdc. *(21 hdc)*

Rnds 2 & 3: Ch 2, hdc in first st and in each st around, join in beg hdc. At end of last rnd, fasten off.

LEG TRIM

Rnd 1: Working in **front lps** *(see Stitch Guide)*, join blue with sc in first st on First Leg, sc in each st around, join in beg sc.

Rnd 2: Ch 1, sc in each st around, join in beg sc. Fasten off.

Rep Leg Trim on 2nd Leg.

Fold Leg Trim up.

BOOTIE
MAKE 2.

Rnd 1: With blue, ch 8, 2 sc in 2nd ch from hook, sc in each of next 4 chs, hdc in next ch, 4 hdc in last ch, working on opposite side of ch, hdc in next ch, sc in each of next 4 chs, 2 sc in last ch, join in beg sc. *(18 sts)*

Rnd 2: Ch 1, 2 sc in first st, sc in each of next 5 sts, hdc in next st, 2 hdc in each of next 4 sts, hdc in next st, sc in each of next 5 sts, 2 sc in last st, join in **back lp** *(see Stitch Guide)* of beg sc. *(24 sts)*

Rnd 3: Working in back lps, ch 1, sc in each st around, join in both lps of beg sc.

Rnd 4: Ch 1, sc in each st around, join in beg sc.

Rnd 5: Ch 1, sc in each of first 8 sts, [sc dec in next 2 sts] 4 times, sc in each of last 8 sts, join in beg sc. *(20 sc)*

Rnd 6: Ch 1, sc in each of first 9 sts, sc dec in next 2 sts, sc in each of last 9 sts, join in beg sc. Fasten off. *(19 sc)*

Rnd 7: Working in back lps, join cream with sc in first st, sc in each of next 6 sts, [sc dec in next 2 sts] 3 times, sc in each of last 6 sts, join in beg sc. *(16 sc)*

Rnd 8: Ch 1, sc in each st around, join in beg sc.

Rnd 9: Working in front lps, ch 1, sc in each st around, join in both lps of beg sc.

Rnd 10: Ch 1, sc in each st around, join in beg sc. Fasten off.

Roll rnds 9 and 10 down for cuff.

HAT

Rnd 1: With cream, ch 2, 6 sc in 2nd ch from hook, join in beg sc. *(6 sc)*

Rnd 2: Ch 2, 2 hdc in first st and in each st around, join in beg hdc. *(12 hdc)*

Rnd 3: Ch 2, 2 hdc in first st, hdc in next st, [2 hdc in next st, hdc in next st] around, join in beg hdc. *(18 hdc)*

Rnd 4: Ch 2, 2 hdc in first st, hdc in each of next 2 sts, [2 hdc in next st, hdc in each of next 2 sts] around, join in beg hdc. *(24 hdc)*

Rnd 5: Ch 2, 2 hdc in first st, hdc in each of next 3 sts, [2 hdc in next st, hdc in each of next 3 sts] around, join in beg hdc. *(30 hdc)*

Rnds 6 & 7: Ch 2, hdc in first st and in each st around, join in beg hdc.

Rnd 8: Ch 2, 2 hdc in first st, hdc in each of next 5 sts, [2 hdc in next st, hdc in each of next 5 sts] around, join in beg hdc. *(35 hdc)*

Rnds 9 & 10: Ch 2, hdc in first st and in each st around, join in beg hdc. At end of last rnd, fasten off.

BRIM

Rnd 1: Working in front lps, join blue in any st, ch 2, hdc in same st and in each st around, join in beg hdc.

Rnd 2: Ch 2, hdc in first st and in each st around, join in beg hdc. Fasten off.

Fold up. ■

Sun Suit

SKILL LEVEL

INTERMEDIATE

FINISHED SIZE

Fits 5-inch baby doll

MATERIALS

- Size 10 crochet cotton:
  150 yds pink
  75 yds white
  20 yds green
- Size 6/1.80mm steel crochet hook or size needed to obtain gauge
- Tapestry needle
- Sewing needle
- White sewing thread
- Small pink pearl beads: 2
- Stitch marker

GAUGE

9 sc = 1 inch; 8 sc rows = 1 inch
15 hdc = 2 inches; 7 hdc rows = 1 inch

PATTERN NOTES

Chain-2 at beginning of row or round does not count as first half double crochet unless otherwise stated.

Join with slip stitch as indicated unless otherwise stated.

INSTRUCTIONS

SUN SUIT

BIB

Row 1 (RS): With pink, ch 10, mark beg ch, hdc in 3rd ch from hook and in each ch across, turn. *(8 hdc)*

Rows 2–4: **Ch 2** *(see Pattern Notes)*, hdc in first st and in each st across, turn.

WAIST

Rnd 5: Now working in rnds, ch 2, hdc in each st across, ch 28, being careful not to twist ch, sl st in first hdc of row 5, do not turn.

Rnd 6: Ch 2, 2 hdc in first st and in each st and in each ch around, **join** *(see Pattern Notes)* in beg hdc. *(72 hdc)*

Rnds 7–9: Ch 2, hdc in first st and in each of next 30 sts, working in **back lps** *(see Stitch Guide)*, hdc in each of next 24 sts, working in both lps, hdc in each of last 17 sts, join in beg hdc.

Rnd 10: Working in both lps, ch 2, hdc in first st and in each st around, join in beg hdc.

FIRST LEG

Rnd 1: Sl st in each of first 12 sts, ch 1, sk first st and each of next 35 sts, sl st in next st, ch 2, hdc in same st and in each of next 23 sts, hdc in each of first 12 sl sts, 2 hdc in next ch, join in beg hdc. *(38 hdc)*

Rnd 2: Ch 2, hdc in first st and in each st around, join in beg hdc.

Rnd 3: Ch 1, **sc dec** *(see Stitch Guide)* in first 2 sts, [sc dec in next 2 sts] around, join in beg sc. *(19 sc)*

Rnd 4: Ch 1, sc in each st around, join in beg sc. Fasten off.

2ND LEG

Rnd 1: With RS facing, join in opposite side of ch-1 in rnd 1 of First Leg, ch 2, 2 hdc in same ch, hdc in each st around, join in beg hdc. *(38 hdc)*

Rnds 2–4: Rep rnds 2–4 of First Leg.

EDGING

With RS facing, join white with sc in any sc of 1 Leg, ch 2, [sc in next st, ch 2] around, join in beg sc. Fasten off.

Rep on rem Leg.

STRAPS & EDGING

With RS facing and white, ch 30 *(first Strap)*, sc in marked ch, work the following steps to complete rnd:

A. Working in starting ch on opposite side of row 1 on Bib, sc in each of next 7 chs, mark last ch you worked in;

B. Ch 31 *(2nd Strap)*, sc in 2nd ch from hook and in each ch across, sc in marked ch;

C. Working down side of Bib, sc in end of each of next 4 rows, sc dec in end of next row and in first ch of ch-28 of Waist;

D. Working on opposite side of starting ch on rnd 5 of Waist, ch 2, [sl st in next ch, ch 2] around, sc dec in last ch and in end of row 5 of Bib;

E. Working up rem side of Bib, sc in end of each of next 4 rows, sc in first st, sc in each of next 30 chs of first Strap. Fasten off.

RUFFLE

Working in rem lps of sts on rnd 6, join white in first st, [ch 3, sl st in next st] across. Fasten off.

Rep on rnds 7 and 8.

HAT

Rnd 1: With pink, ch 2, 6 sc in 2nd ch from hook, join in beg sc. *(6 sc)*

Rnd 2: Ch 2, (hdc, ch 1) twice in first st and in each st around, join in beg hdc.

Rnd 3: Sl st in first ch sp, ch 2, (hdc, ch 1) twice in same ch sp and in each ch sp around, join in beg hdc.

Rnds 4–8: Sl st in first ch sp, ch 2, hdc in same ch sp, ch 1, [hdc in next ch sp, ch 1] around, join in beg hdc.

Rnd 9: Ch 1, sc in first ch sp, *sk next st, (dc, {ch 1, dc} twice) in next ch sp, sk next st**, sc in next ch sp, rep from * around, ending last rep at **, join in beg sc. Fasten off.

RIGHT FLIP-FLOP

Rnd 1 (RS): With pink, ch 8, 2 sc in 2nd ch from hook, sc in each of next 4 chs, hdc in next ch, 4 hdc in last ch, working on opposite side of ch, hdc in next ch, sc in each of next 4 chs, 2 sc in last ch, join in beg sc. *(18 sts)*

Rnd 2: Ch 1, 2 sc in first st and in each of next 3 sts, mark last st worked in as A, sc in each of next 2 sts, hdc in next st, 2 hdc in each of next 3 sts, mark last st worked in as B, 2 hdc in next st, hdc in next st, sc in each of next 3 sts, mark last st worked in as C, sc in each of next 2 sts, 2 sc in last st, join in beg sc. Fasten off.

STRAP

With WS facing, join pink in back lp of marked st A, ch 8, sl st in back lp of marked st B, ch 6, sc in back lp of marked st C, ch 6, sc in back lp of A, join in beg sl st. Fasten off.

LEFT FLIP-FLOP

Rnd 1 (RS): With pink, ch 8, 2 sc in 2nd ch from hook, sc in each of next 4 chs, hdc in next ch, 4 hdc in last ch, working on opposite side of ch, hdc in next ch, sc in each of next 4 chs, 2 sc in last ch, join in beg sc. *(18 sts)*

Rnd 2: Ch 1, 2 sc in first st, sc in each of next 4 sts, mark last st worked in A, sc in each of next 2 sts, hdc in next st, 2 hdc in next st, hdc in next st, mark last st worked in B, hdc in same st, 2 hdc in each of next 2 sts, hdc in next st, sc in each of next 3 sts, mark last st worked in C, sc in each of next 2 sts, 2 sc in last st, join in beg sc. Fasten off.

STRAP

With WS facing, join pink with sl st in back lp of marked st A, ch 6, sl st in back lp of marked st B, ch 8, sc in back lp of marked st C, ch 6, sc in back lp of A, join in beg sl st. Fasten off.

FLOWER
MAKE 2.

Rnd 1: With white, ch 2, 6 sc in 2nd ch from hook, join in beg sc. *(6 sc)*

Rnd 2: Ch 1, (sc, 2 dc, sc) in each st around, join in beg sc. Leaving long end, fasten off. *(6 petals)*

LEAF
MAKE 4.

With green, ch 7, dc in 4th ch from hook, hdc in next ch, sc in next ch, 3 sc in last ch, working on opposite side of ch, sc in next ch, hdc in next ch, dc in next ch, ch 2, sl st in next ch. Leaving long end, fasten off.

FINISHING

1. Sew 1 Flower and 2 Leaves to Hat as shown in photo.

2. Sew 1 pearl bead to center of Flower.

3. Sew 1 Flower and 2 Leaves to Sun Suit as shown in photo.

4. Sew 1 pearl bead to center of Flower. ■

Cuddle-Up Romper

SKILL LEVEL

INTERMEDIATE

FINISHED SIZE

Fits 5-inch baby doll

MATERIALS

- Size 10 crochet cotton:
  200 yds white
  75 yds pink
- Size 6/1.80mm steel crochet hook or size needed to obtain gauge
- Tapestry needle
- Sewing needle
- White sewing thread
- 1/8-inch pink ribbon:
  2 6-inch pieces
  1 12-inch piece
- Ribbon roses: 2
- Small snap
- Stitch marker

GAUGE

9 sc = 1 inch; 8 sc rows = 1 inch
15 hdc = 2 inches; 7 hdc rows = 1 inch

PATTERN NOTES

Chain-2 at beginning of row or round does not count as first half double crochet unless otherwise stated.

Chain-3 at beginning of row or round counts as first double crochet unless otherwise stated.

Join with slip stitch as indicated unless otherwise stated.

SPECIAL STITCH

Shell: (2 dc, ch 1, 2 dc) in place indicated.

INSTRUCTIONS

BLOUSE

Row 1: Beg at neck, with pink, ch 29, 2 sc in 2nd ch from hook and in each ch across, turn. *(56 sc)*

Row 2 (RS): Ch 1, sc in each of first 8 sts, ch 7, sk next 12 sts *(armhole)*, sc in each of next 16 sts, ch 7, sk next 12 sts *(armhole)*, sc in each of last 8 sts, turn.

Row 3: Ch 1, sc in each st and in each ch across. Fasten off. *(46 sc)*

Row 4 (Ribbon row): With RS facing and neck facing down, **join** *(see Pattern Notes)* white in first st, **ch 2** *(see Pattern Notes)*, hdc in same st, [ch 1, sk next st, hdc in next st] across, hdc in last st, turn.

Row 5: **Ch 3** *(see Pattern Notes)*, sk next st and ch sp, 3 dc in next st, [sk next ch sp, dc in next st, sk next ch sp, **shell** *(see Special Stitch)* in next st, sk next ch sp, dc in next st, sk next ch sp, 3 dc in next st] across, ending with dc in top of beg ch-2 on row 4, turn.

Row 6: Ch 3, sk next st, shell in next st, sk next st, [**fpdc** *(see Stitch Guide)* around next st, sk next 2 sts, 3 dc in ch sp of next shell, sk next 2 sts, fpdc around next st, sk next st, shell in next st, sk next st] across, ending with dc in last st, turn.

Row 7: Ch 3, sk next 2 sts, 3 dc in ch sp of next shell, sk next 2 sts, [**bpdc** *(see Stitch Guide)* around next st, sk next st, shell in next st, sk next st, bpdc around next st, sk next 2 sts, 3 dc in ch sp of next shell, sk next 2 sts] across, ending with dc in last st, turn.

Row 8: Ch 1, sc in first st, sk next st, 5 dc in next st, sk next st, sc in next st, [sk next 2 sts, 5 dc in ch sp of next shell, sk next 2 sts, sc in next st, sk next st, 5 dc in next st, sk next st, sc in next st] across. Fasten off.

EDGING

With RS facing, join pink in first st, *sc in next st, [ch 2, sc in next st] 4 times, sl st in next st, rep from * across. Fasten off.

SLEEVES

Rnd 1: Join white in center ch of ch-7 of 1 armhole, ch 2, hdc in same ch and in each of next 3 chs, hdc in end of row 2, 2 hdc in each of next sk 12 sts, hdc in end of row 2, hdc in each of last 3 chs, join in beg hdc. *(33 hdc)*

Rnds 2 & 3: Ch 2, hdc in first st and in each st around, join in beg hdc.

Rnd 4: Ch 1, **sc dec** *(see Stitch Guide)* in first 2 sts, [sc dec in next 2 sts] around, ending with sc in last st, join in beg sc.

Rnd 5: Ch 1, sc in each st around, join in beg sc. Fasten off.

Rep Sleeve in rem armhole.

EDGING

Join pink in first st, ch 2, [sl st in next st, ch 2] around, join in beg sl st. Fasten off.

Rep on rem Sleeve.

FINISHING

1. Sew snap to ends of row 1 at neck edge.

2. Weave 1 6-inch piece of ribbon through row 4, beg at back edge and ending in front. Turn end under at back edge and tack in place. Rep with rem 6-inch piece on other side of row 4. Tie ends of 6-inch pieces in bow.

3. Sew 1 ribbon rose to front as shown in photo.

PANTS

FIRST LEG

Rnd 1: Beg at bootie, with white, ch 8, 2 sc in 2nd ch from hook, sc in each of next 4 chs, hdc in next ch, 4 hdc in last ch, working on opposite side of ch, hdc in next ch, sc in each of next 4 chs, 2 sc in last ch, join in beg sc. *(18 sts)*

Rnd 2: Ch 1, 2 sc in first st, sc in each of next 5 sts, hdc in next st, 2 hdc in each of next 4 sts, hdc in next st, sc in each of next 5 sts, 2 sc in last st, join in **back lp** *(see Stitch Guide)* of beg sc. *(24 sts)*

Rnd 3: Working in back lps, ch 1, sc in each st around, join in both lps of beg sc.

Rnd 4: Ch 1, sc in each st around, join in beg sc.

Rnd 5: Ch 1, sc in each of first 8 sts, [sc dec in next 2 sts] 4 times, sc in each of last 8 sts, join in beg sc. *(20 sc)*

Rnd 6: Ch 1, sc in each of first 9 sts, sc dec in next 2 sts, sc in each of last 9 sts, join in beg sc. *(19 sc)*

Rnd 7: Ch 1, sc in each of first 7 sts, [sc dec in next 2 sts] 3 times, sc in each of last 6 sts, join in beg sc. *(16 sc)*

Rnd 8: Ch 1, sc in each st around, join in beg sc.

Rnd 9: Ch 2, 2 hdc in first st and in each st around, join in beg hdc. *(32 hdc)*

Rnds 10–12: Ch 2, hdc in first st and in each st around, join in beg hdc.

Rnd 13: Ch 2, hdc in first st and in each of next 27 sts, mark last st for joining of Legs, hdc in each st around, join in beg hdc. Fasten off.

2ND LEG

Rnds 1–12: Rep rnds 1–12 of First Leg.

Rnd 13: Ch 2, hdc in first st and in each st around, join in beg hdc. Do not fasten off.

CONNECTING LEGS

Rnd 14: Ch 2, hdc in first st, hdc in each of next 10 sts, leaving rem sts unworked for now, holding both Legs tog with toes pointing in the same direction, hdc in marked hdc of First Leg, hdc in each of next 31 sts, hdc in same marked st, yo, insert hook in sp between 11th st of 2nd Leg and first hdc of First Leg, pull lp through, hdc in same st as 11th hdc of 2nd Leg, pulling through all lps on hook *(this will close hole between Legs)*, hdc in rem hdc of 2nd Leg, join in first hdc of 2nd Leg. *(66 hdc)*

Rnd 15: Ch 2, hdc in first st and in each st around, join in beg hdc.

Rnd 16: Ch 2, **hdc dec** *(see Stitch Guide)* in first 2 sts, hdc in each of next 2 sts, *hdc dec in next 2 sts, hdc in each of next 2 sts, rep from * around, ending last rep with hdc in each of last 2 sts, join in beg hdc dec. *(50 hdc)*

Rnd 17: Ch 2, hdc in first st and in each st around, join in beg hdc.

Rnd 18: Rep rnd 16. *(38 hdc)*

Rnds 19–21: Ch 2, hdc in first st and in each st around, join in beg hdc. At end of last rnd, fasten off.

Pants will be baggy like soft baby romper pants, but they should stay on when you hold the doll up.

WAIST EDGING

Join pink in any st, ch 2, [sl st in next st, ch 2] around, join in beg sl st. Fasten off.

BOOTIE EDGING

Join pink in rem lps of rnd 2 of 1 Pants Leg, ch 1, [sl st in next st, ch 1, around, join in beg sl st. Fasten off.

Rep on rem Leg.

HEADBAND

With white, ch 36, being careful not to twist ch, sl st in first ch to form ring, try on head for fit, add or dec number of ch to fit, make sure to have even number of chs, ch 2, hdc in first ch, ch 1, sk next ch, [hdc in next ch, ch 1, sk next ch] around, join in beg hdc. Fasten off.

EDGING

Rnd 1: Join pink in any st, ch 2, *sl st in next ch sp, ch 2**, sl st in next st, ch 2, rep from * around, ending last rep at **, join in beg sl st. Fasten off.

Rnd 2: Working in starting ch on opposite side of Headband, join pink in any ch, ch 2, [sl st in next ch, ch 2] around, join in beg sl st. Fasten off.

Weave ribbon around Headband. Tie ends in bow.

Sew ribbon rose to center of bow. ■

Cherry **Swimsuit**

SKILL LEVEL

INTERMEDIATE

FINISHED SIZE

Fits 5-inch baby doll

MATERIALS

- Size 10 crochet cotton:
  100 yds white
  50 yds red
  1 yd brown
- Size 6/1.80mm steel crochet hook or size needed to obtain gauge
- Tapestry needle
- Sewing needle
- Red sewing thread
- Stitch marker

GAUGE

9 sc = 1 inch; 8 sc rows = 1 inch
15 hdc = 2 inches; 7 hdc rows = 1 inch

PATTERN NOTES

Chain-2 at beginning of row or round does not count as first half double crochet unless otherwise stated.

Chain-3 at beginning of row or round counts as first double crochet unless otherwise stated.

Join with slip stitch as indicated unless otherwise stated.

INSTRUCTIONS

SWIMSUIT

PANTY FRONT

Row 1: With white, ch 4, sc in 2nd ch from hook and in each ch across, turn. *(3 sc)*

Row 2: Ch 1, sc in each st across, turn.

Rows 3–10: Ch 1, 2 sc in first st, sc in each st across with 2 sc in last st, turn. At end of last row, fasten off. *(19 sc at end of last row)*

PANTY BACK

Row 1: With WS facing and working in starting ch on opposite side of row 1 on Panty Front, join white with sc in first ch, sc in each ch across, turn. *(3 sc)*

Row 2: Ch 1, sc in each st across, turn.

Rows 3–11: Ch 1, 2 sc in first st, sc in each st across with 2 sc in last st, turn. At end of last row, do not fasten off. *(21 sc at end of last row)*

PANTY TOP

Rnd 12: Now working in rnds, ch 1, 2 sc in first st, sc in each st across with 2 sc in last st, sc in first st of row 10 on Panty Front, sc in each st across, **join** *(see Pattern Notes)* in beg sc. *(42 sc)*

Last rnd: Ch 1, sc in first st, mark this st, sc in each st around, join in beg sc.

SKIRT

Rnd 1: Working in **front lps** *(see Stitch Guide)*, ch 4 *(counts as first tr)*, tr in same st, 2 tr in each st around, join in 4th ch of beg ch-4. Fasten off. *(84 tr)*

EDGING

Rnd 2: Join red with sc in any st, ch 1, [sc in next st, ch 1] around, join in beg sc. Fasten off.

TOP

Rnd 1 (RS): Working in rem lps of Panty Top, join white with sc in marked st, sc in each st around, join in beg sc.

Row 2: Now working in rows, sl st in each of next 11 sts, sc in each of next 40 sts, including some of first sl st, leaving rem sts unworked, turn.

Row 3: Ch 1, sk first st, sc in each of next 38 sts, leaving last st unworked, turn. *(38 sc)*

Row 4: Ch 1, sk first st, sl st in each of next 2 sts, sc in each of next 3 sts, **sc dec** *(see Stitch Guide)* in next 2 sts, [sc in each of next 4 sts, sc dec in next 2 sts] 4 times, sc in each of next 3 sts, sl st in next st, leaving rem sts unworked, turn. *(27 sc)*

Row 5: Ch 1, sk first sl st, sl st in each of next 2 sts, sc in each of next 3 sts, [sc dec in next 2 sts, sc in each of next 3 sts] 4 times, sl st in next st, leaving rem sts unworked. Fasten off.

Row 6: With RS facing, counting from right to left, join white in 6th st, sc in each of next 10 sts, sl st in next st, leaving rem sts unworked, turn.

Row 7: Sk sl st, sl st in next st, sc in each of next 8 sts, sl st in next st, leaving rem sts unworked, turn.

Row 8: Ch 1, sk sl st, sc in each sc across, leaving last sl st unworked, turn.

Row 9: Ch 1, sc in first st, mark this st A, sc in each of next 7 sts, mark last st B. Fasten off.

STRAPS & EDGING

With red, ch 30 *(strap)*, sl st in marked A st, evenly sp sc in ends of rows and across back and in ends of rows back up to marked B st, ch 31 *(strap)*, sc in 2nd ch from hook and in each ch across, sc in marked B st, sc in each of next 6 sts, sc in marked A st, sc in each of first 30 chs. Fasten off.

LEG EDGING

Join red with sc at side of row 1 of Panties, evenly sp 23 sc around 1 leg opening, join in beg sc. Fasten off. *(24 sc)*

Rep on rem leg opening.

CHERRY
MAKE 2.

With red, ch 2, 6 sc in 2nd ch from hook, join in beg sc. Leaving long end, fasten off.

FINISHING

1. Sew Cherries to front of Swimsuit as shown in photo.

2. Using **straight stitch** *(see Fig. 1)* with brown, embroider stems as shown in photo.

Fig. 1
Straight Stitch

SUN VISOR

Rnd 1: With white, ch 35, being careful not to twist ch, sl st in first ch to form ring, ch 1, sc in each ch around, join in beg sc. *(35 sc)*

Rnd 2: Ch 1, sc in each st around, join in beg sc.

Row 3 (Visor): Ch 1, sc in first st, hdc in next st, 2 dc in each of next 8 sts, hdc in next st, sc in next st, sl st in next st, leaving rem sts unworked. Fasten off.

TOP EDGING

Working in starting ch on opposite side of rnd 1, join red with sc in any ch, sc in each ch around, join in beg sc. Fasten off.

BOTTOM EDGING

Join red with sc in st to right of first sc on Visor, sc in each st around, join in beg sc. Fasten off.

SANDAL
MAKE 2.
SOLE

Rnd 1: With red, ch 8, 2 sc in 2nd ch from hook, sc in each of next 4 chs, hdc in next ch, 4 hdc in last ch, working on opposite side of ch, hdc in next ch, sc in each of next 4 chs, 2 sc in last ch, join in beg sc. *(18 sts)*

Rnd 2: Ch 1, 2 sc in first st, sc in each of next 5 sts, hdc in next st, 2 hdc in each of next 4 sts, hdc in next st, sc in each of next 5 sts, 2 sc in last st, join in **back lp** *(see Stitch Guide)* of beg sc. Fasten off. *(24 sts)*

HEEL

Row 1: With edge of Heel facing, working in back lps, join red with sc in 4th st to right of joining, sc in each of next 7 sts, leaving rem sts unworked, turn. *(8 sc)*

Row 2: Ch 1, sc in each st across, turn.

Rnd 3: Now working in rnds, ch 1, sc in each of first 3 sts, sc dec in next 2 sts, sc in each of next 3 sts, ch 8 *(strap)*, join in beg sc.

Rnd 4: Ch 1, sc in each st around, join in beg sc. Fasten off.

FRONT STRAP

With Heel and inside of Sole facing, sk 3 sts to right of Heel on side, join red in **front lp** *(see Stitch Guide)* of next st, ch 6, sl st in front lp of 4th st from left side of Heel on opposite side, sl st in back lp of next st towards toe, turn. Sc in each ch across, sl st in next st on Sole towards toe on opposite side of Sole. Fasten off. ■

Spring Dress & Jacket

SKILL LEVEL

INTERMEDIATE

FINISHED SIZE

Fits 5-inch baby doll

MATERIALS

- Size 10 crochet cotton:
  200 yds variegated
  100 yds pink
  25 yds white
- Size 6/1.80mm steel crochet hook or size needed to obtain gauge
- Tapestry needle
- Sewing needle
- White sewing thread
- Small button
- Ribbon roses: 2
- Small snap

GAUGE

9 sc = 1 inch; 8 sc rows = 1 inch
15 hdc = 2 inches; 7 hdc rows = 1 inch

PATTERN NOTES

Chain-2 at beginning of row or round does not count as first half double crochet unless otherwise stated.

Chain-3 at beginning of row or round counts as first double crochet unless otherwise stated.

Join with slip stitch as indicated unless otherwise stated.

SPECIAL STITCH

Shell: 3 dc in place indicated.

INSTRUCTIONS

DRESS

Row 1: Beg at neck, with variegated, ch 29, 2 sc in 2nd ch from hook and in each ch across, turn. *(56 sc)*

Row 2: Ch 1, sc in each of first 8 sts, ch 6, sk next 12 sts *(armhole)*, sc in each of next 16 sts, ch 6, sk next 12 sts *(armhole)*, sc in each of last 8 sts, turn.

Row 3: Ch 1, sc in each st and in each ch across, turn. *(44 sc)*

Rows 4 & 5: Ch 1, sc in each st across, turn.

Row 6: Ch 1, sc in first st, *__shell__ *(see Special Stitch)* in next st**, sc in next st, rep from * across, ending last rep at **, turn. *(22 sc, 22 shells)*

Row 7: Working in **front lps** *(see Stitch Guide)*, sl st in first st, ch 1, sc in next st, sk next st, *shell in next sc**, sc in center dc of next shell, rep from * across, ending last rep at **, turn.

Rnd 8: Now working in rnds and in **back lps** *(see Stitch Guide)*, sl st in first st, ch 1, sc in next st, *shell in next sc**, sc in center dc of next shell, rep from * around, ending last rep at **, **join** *(see Pattern Notes)* in beg sc.

Rnd 9: Working in back lps, **ch 3** *(see Pattern Notes)*, 2 dc in same st, *sc in center dc of next shell**, shell in next sc, around, rep from * around, ending last rep at **, join in 3rd ch of beg ch-3.

Rnd 10: Working in back lps, sl st in next st, ch 1, sc in same st, *shell in next sc**, sc in center dc of next shell, rep from * around, ending last rep at **, join in beg sc.

Rnds 11 & 12 or to desired length: Rep rnds 9 and 10. At end of last rnd, fasten off.

Sew 1 ribbon rose to top center as shown in photo.

Sew snap to top of back opening on Dress.

JACKET

Row 1: Beg at neck, with pink, ch 30, 2 hdc in 3rd ch from hook and in each ch across, turn. *(56 hdc)*

Row 2: **Ch 2** *(see Pattern Notes),* hdc in first st and in each of next 7 sts, ch 7, sk next 12 sts *(armhole),* hdc in each of next 16 sts, ch 7, sk next 12 sts *(armhole),* hdc in each of last 8 sts, turn.

Row 3: Ch 2, hdc in first st and in each st and in each ch across, turn. *(46 hdc)*

Row 4: Ch 2, hdc in first st and in each st across, turn.

EDGING

Working in back lps along bottom edge, ch 1, sc in first st, [ch 2, sc in next st] across, working up side in ends of rows, sc in end of each of next 4 rows to neck, working in starting ch on opposite side of row 1, sl st in first ch, [ch 1, sl st in next ch] across, working down rem side in ends of rows, (sc, ch 3, sc) in end of first row *(button lp),* sc in end of each of next 3 rows, join in beg sc. Fasten off.

Sew button to front opposite button lp.

SLEEVES

Rnd 1: Join pink in center ch of ch-7 on 1 armhole, ch 2, hdc in same ch, hdc in each of next 3 chs, hdc in end of row 2, hdc in each of next 12 sk sts, hdc in end of row 2, hdc in each of last 3 chs, join in beg hdc. *(21 hdc)*

Rnds 2–6: Ch 2, hdc in first st and in each st around, join in beg hdc.

Rnd 7: Ch 1, **sc dec** *(see Stitch Guide)* in first 2 sts, sc in next st, [sc dec in next 2 sts, sc in next st] around, join in beg sc dec.

Rnd 8: Working in front lps, ch 1, sc in first st, ch 2, [sc in next st, ch 2] around, join in beg sc. Fasten off.

Rep in rem armhole.

PANTIES
FRONT

Row 1: With variegated, ch 4, sc in 2nd ch from hook and in each ch across, turn. *(3 sc)*

Row 2 (RS): Ch 1, sc in each st across, turn.

Rows 3–10: Ch 1, 2 sc in first st, sc in each st across with 2 sc in last st, turn. At end of last row, fasten off. *(19 sc at end of last row)*

BACK

Row 1: Working in starting ch on opposite side of row 1 on Front, join variegated with sc in first ch, sc in each ch across, turn. *(3 sc)*

Row 2: Ch 1, sc in each st across, turn.

Rows 3–11: Ch 1, 2 sc in first st, sc in each st across with 2 sc in last st, turn. *(21 sc at end of last row)*

Rnd 12: Joining Front and Back tog, ch 1, 2 sc in first st, sc in each st across Back with 2 sc in last st, sc in first st on Front, sc in each st across, join in beg sc. Fasten off.

LEG EDGING

Join variegated with sc in side of beg ch, evenly sp 23 sc around, join in beg sc. Fasten off. *(24 sc)*

Rep on rem Leg opening.

BOOTIE

MAKE 2.

Rnd 1: Beg at sole, with pink, ch 8, 2 sc in 2nd ch from hook, sc in each of next 4 chs, hdc in next ch, 4 hdc in last ch, working on opposite side of ch, hdc in next ch, sc in each of next 4 chs, 2 sc in last ch, join in beg sc. *(18 sts)*

Rnd 2: Ch 1, 2 sc in first st, sc in each of next 5 sts, hdc in next st, 2 hdc in each of next 4 sts, hdc in next st, sc in each of next 5 sts, 2 sc in last st, join in back lp of beg sc. *(24 sts)*

Rnd 3: Working in back lps, ch 1, sc in each st around, join in both lps of beg sc.

Rnd 4: Ch 1, sc in each st around, join in beg sc.

Rnd 5: Ch 1, sc in each of first 8 sts, [sc dec in next 2 sts] 4 times, sc in each of last 8 sts, join in beg sc. Fasten off. *(20 sc)*

SOCK

Rnd 6: Working in back lps, join white with sc in first st, sc in each of next 8 sts, sc dec in next 2 sts, sc in each of last 9 sts, join in beg sc. *(19 sc)*

Rnd 7: Ch 1, sc in each of first 6 sts, [sc dec in next 2 sts] 3 times, sc in each of last 6 sts, join in beg sc. *(16 sc)*

Rnd 8: Ch 1, sc in each st around, join in back lp of beg sc.

Rnd 9: Working in back lps, ch 3, dc in each st around, join in 3rd ch of beg ch-3. Fasten off.

STRAP

Working in rem lps of rnd 5, join pink with sc in first st, sc in each of next 5 sts, ch 8, sk next 8 sts, sc in each of last 6 sts, join in beg sc. Fasten off.

SOCK RUFFLE

Working in rem lps on rnd 8, join variegated in any st, ch 3, [sl st in next st, ch 3] around, join in beg sl st. Fasten off.

HEADBAND

Rnd 1: With variegated, ch 35, being careful not to twist ch, sl st in first ch to form ring, ch 1, sc in each ch around, join in beg sc. *(35 sc)*

Rnd 2: Ch 1, sc in first st, sc in each st around, join in beg sc.

EDGING

Ch 3, [sl st in next st, ch 3] around, join in joining sl st of last rnd. Fasten off.

Working in starting ch on opposite side of rnd 1, join variegated with sl st in any ch, ch 3, [sl st in next ch, ch 3] around, join in beg sl st. Fasten off.

Sew rem ribbon rose to Headband as shown in photo. ■

Wine & Roses Romper

SKILL LEVEL

INTERMEDIATE

FINISHED SIZE
Fits 5-inch baby doll

MATERIALS
- Size 10 crochet cotton:
  200 yds cream
  25 yds burgundy
- Size 6/1.80mm steel crochet hook or size needed to obtain gauge
- Tapestry needle
- Sewing needle
- Cream sewing thread
- Ribbon roses: 2
- Small snap

GAUGE
9 sc = 1 inch; 8 sc rows = 1 inch
15 hdc = 2 inches; 7 hdc rows = 1 inch

PATTERN NOTES
Chain-2 at beginning of row or round does not count as first half double crochet unless otherwise stated.

Chain-3 at beginning of row or round counts as first double crochet unless otherwise stated.

Join with slip stitch as indicated unless otherwise stated.

INSTRUCTIONS
ROMPER
Row 1: Beg at neck, with burgundy, ch 29, 2 sc in 2nd ch from hook and in each ch across, turn. *(56 sc)*

Row 2 (RS): Ch 1, sc in each of first 8 sts, ch 7, sk next 12 sts *(armhole)*, sc in each of next 16 sts, ch 7, sk next 12 sts *(armhole)*, sc in each of last 8 sts, turn.

Row 3: Ch 1, sc in each st and in each ch across, turn. *(46 sc)*

Row 4: Ch 1, sc in each st across, turn. Fasten off.

Row 5: Join cream with sc in first st, sc in same st, sc in next st, [2 sc in next st, sc in next st] across, turn. *(69 sc)*

Row 6: Ch 1, sc in first st, [dc in next st, sc in next st] across, turn.

Row 7: **Ch 3** *(see Pattern Notes)*, [sc in next dc, dc in next sc] across, turn.

Rnd 8: Now working in rnds, ch 1, sc in first dc, [dc in next sc, sc in next dc] around, sk first sc, **join** *(see Pattern Notes)* in beg dc. *(68 sts)*

Rnd 9: Ch 1, sc in first dc, dc in next sc, [sc in next dc, dc in next sc] around, join in beg sc.

Rnd 10: Ch 3, *sc in next dc**, dc in next sc, rep from * around, ending last rep at **, join in 3rd ch of beg ch-3.

Rnds 11–14: [Rep rnds 9 and 10 alternately] twice.

FIRST LEG

Rnd 1 (RS): Ch 2 *(see Pattern Notes)*, sk first 34 sts, sl st in next st, ch 1, sc in same dc, dc in next sc, [sc in next dc, dc in next sc] around to beg ch-2, sc in next ch, dc in next ch, join in beg sc. *(36 sts)*

Rnd 2: Ch 3, *sc in next dc**, dc in next sc, rep from * around, ending last rep at **, join in 3rd ch of beg ch-3.

Rnd 3: Ch 1, sc in first dc, *dc in next sc**, sc in next dc, rep from * around, ending last rep at **, join in beg sc.

Rnds 4–7: [Rep rnds 2 and 3 alternately] twice.

Rnd 8: Ch 1, **sc dec** *(see Stitch Guide)* in first 2 sts, [sc dec in next 2 sts] around, join in beg sc dec. *(18 sc)*

Rnd 9: Ch 1, sc in each st around, join in beg sc. Fasten off.

EDGING

Join burgundy with sc in any st, sc in each st around, join in beg sc. Fasten off.

2ND LEG

Rnd 1: With RS facing, join cream with sc in first st on rnd 14 *(should be first ch-3)*, dc in next sc, [sc in next dc, dc in next sc] around to ch-2, working on opposite side of ch-2, sc in first ch, dc in last ch, join in beg sc.

Rnds 2–9: Rep rows 2–9 of First Leg.

EDGING

Join burgundy with sc in any st, sc in each st around, join in beg sc. Fasten off.

SLEEVES

Rnd 1: Join cream with sc in center ch of ch-7 at 1 armhole, sc in each of next 3 chs, 2 sc in end of row 2, sc in each of next 12 sk sts, 2 sc in end of row 2, sc in each of last 3 chs, join in beg sc. *(22 sc)*

Rnd 2: Ch 1, sc in first st, dc in next st, [sc in next st, dc in next st] around, join in beg sc.

Rnd 3: Ch 3, sc in next dc, [dc in next sc, sc in next dc] around, join in 3rd ch of beg ch-3.

Rnd 4: Ch 1, sc in first st, dc in next sc, [sc in next dc, dc in next sc] around, join in beg sc.

Rnd 5: Rep rnd 3.

Rnd 6: Ch 1, sc dec in first 2 sts, [sc dec in next 2 sts] around, join in beg sc dec. Fasten off.

EDGING

Join burgundy with sc in any st, sc in each st around, join in beg sc. Fasten off.

Rep on rem armhole.

FINISHING

1. Sew snap to Romper at neck.

2. Sew 1 ribbon rose to front as shown in photo.

HAT

Rnd 1: With cream, ch 2, 6 sc in 2nd ch from hook, join in beg sc. *(6 sc)*

Rnd 2: Ch 1, 2 sc in each st around, join in beg sc. *(12 sc)*

Rnd 3: Ch 1, 2 sc in first st, sc in next st, [2 sc in next st, sc in next st] around, join in beg sc. *(18 sc)*

Rnd 4: Ch 1, 2 sc in first st, sc in each of next 2 sts, [2 sc in next st, sc in each of next 2 sts] around, join in beg sc. *(24 sc)*

Rnd 5: Ch 1, 2 sc in first st, sc in each of next 3 sts, [2 sc in next st, sc in each of next 3 sts] around, join in beg sc. *(30 sc)*

Rnd 6: Ch 1, 2 sc in first st, sc in each of next 4 sts, [2 sc in next st, sc in each of next 4 sts] around, join in beg sc. *(36 sc)*

Rnd 7: Ch 1, 2 sc in first st, sc in each of next 5 sts, [2 sc in next st, sc in each of next 5 sts] around, join in beg sc. *(42 sc)*

Rnd 8: Ch 1, 2 sc in first st, sc in each of next 6 sts, [2 sc in next st, sc in each of next 6 sts] around, join in beg sc. *(48 sc)*

Rnd 9: Ch 1, 2 sc in first st, sc in each of next 7 sts, [2 sc in next st, sc in each of next 7 sts] around, join in beg sc. *(54 sc)*

Rnd 10: Ch 1, 2 sc in first st, sc in each of next 8 sts, [2 sc in next st, sc in each of next 8 sts] around, join in beg sc. *(60 sc)*

Rnd 11: Ch 1, sc in first st, dc in next st, [sc in next st, dc in next st] around, join in beg sc.

Rnd 12: Ch 3, sc in next dc, [dc in next sc, sc in next dc] around, join in 3rd ch of beg ch-3.

Rnd 13: Ch 1, sc in first dc, dc in next sc, [sc in next dc, dc in next sc] around, join in beg sc.

Rnd 14: Rep rnd 12.

Rnd 15: Ch 1, sc dec in first 2 sts, sc in next st, [sc dec in next 2 sts, sc in next st] around, join in beg sc. *(40 sc)*

Rnds 16–18: Ch 1, sc in each st around, join in beg sc. At end of last rnd, fasten off.

EDGING

Join burgundy with sc in any st, sc in each st around, join in beg sc. Fasten off.

Sew rem ribbon rose to Hat as shown in photo.

SHOE

MAKE 2.

Rnd 1: Beg at sole, with burgundy, ch 8, 2 sc in 2nd ch from hook, sc in each of next 4 chs, hdc in next ch, 4 hdc in last ch, working on opposite side of ch, hdc in next ch, sc in each of next 4 chs, 2 sc in last ch, join in beg sc. *(18 sts)*

Rnd 2: Ch 1, 2 sc in first st, sc in each of next 5 sts, hdc in next st, 2 hdc in each of next 4 sts, hdc in next st, sc in each of next 5 sts, 2 sc in last st, join in **back lp** *(see Stitch Guide)* of beg sc. *(24 sts)*

Rnd 3: Working in back lps, ch 1, sc in each st around, join in both lps of beg sc.

Rnd 4: Ch 1, sc in each st around, join in beg sc.

Rnd 5: Ch 1, sc in each of first 8 sts, [sc dec in next 2 sts] 4 times, sc in each of last 8 sts, join in beg sc. *(20 sc)*

Rnd 6: Ch 1, sc in each of first 6 sts, ch 8 *(strap)*, sk next 8 sc, sc in each of last 6 sts, join in beg sc. Fasten off. ■

Lucy's Sunday Meeting **Dress**

SKILL LEVEL

INTERMEDIATE

FINISHED SIZE

Fits 5-inch baby doll

MATERIALS

- Size 10 crochet cotton:
  200 yds lavender
  100 yds white
- Size 6/1.80mm steel crochet hook or size needed to obtain gauge
- Tapestry needle
- Sewing needle
- White sewing thread
- Lavender ribbon roses: 2
- Small snap

GAUGE

9 sc = 1 inch; 8 sc rows = 1 inch
15 hdc = 2 inches; 7 hdc rows = 1 inch

PATTERN NOTES

Chain-2 at beginning of row or round does not count as first half double crochet unless otherwise stated.

Chain-3 at beginning of row or round counts as first double crochet unless otherwise stated.

Join with slip stitch as indicated unless otherwise stated.

SPECIAL STITCHES

Beginning shell (beg shell): Ch 3, (dc, ch 2, 2 dc) in place indicated.

Shell: (2 dc, ch 2, 2 dc) in place indicated.

Fan: (Dc, (ch 1, dc) 5 times) in place indicated.

INSTRUCTIONS

DRESS

Row 1 (WS): Beg at neck, with white, ch 29, 2 sc in 2nd ch from hook and in each ch across, turn. *(56 sc)*

Rows 2–4: Ch 1, sc in each st across, turn.

Row 5: Ch 1, sc in each of first 8 sts, ch 7, sk next 12 sts *(armhole)*, sc in each of next 16 sts, ch 7, sk next 12 sts *(armhole)*, sc in each of last 8 sts, turn.

Row 6: Ch 1, sc in each st and in each ch across, turn. Fasten off. *(46 sc)*

Row 7: **Join** *(see Pattern Notes)* lavender in first st, **ch 3** *(see Pattern Notes)*, (dc, ch 2, 2 dc) in same st, [sk next st, dc in next st, sk next st, **shell** *(see Special Stitches)* in next st] across, leaving last st unworked, turn. *(11 dc, 12 shells)*

Row 8: Sl st in each of first 2 sts and first ch sp, **beg shell** *(see Special Stitches)* in same ch sp,[sk next 2 dc of shell, **fpdc** *(see Stitch Guide)* around next dc, shell in ch sp of next shell] across, turn.

Row 9: Sl st in each of first 2 sts and ch sp, beg shell in same ch sp, [sk next 2 dc of shell, **bpdc** *(see Stitch Guide)* around fpdc, shell in ch sp of next shell] across, turn.

Rnd 10: Now working in rnds, sl st in each of first 2 sts and ch sp, beg shell in same ch sp, [fpdc around next bpdc, shell in ch sp of next shell] around, join in 3rd ch of beg ch-3.

Rnd 11: Sl st in next st and ch sp, beg shell in same ch sp, [fpdc around next fpdc, shell in ch sp of next shell] around, dc in sp between last shell and first shell, join in 3rd ch of beg ch-3.

Rnd 12: Sl st in next dc and ch sp, beg shell in same ch sp, fpdc around next fpdc, shell in ch sp of next shell] around, fpdc around last dc, join in 3rd ch of beg ch-3. Fasten off. *(12 fpdc, 12 shells)*

Rnd 13: With RS facing, join white with sc in any fpdc, *****fan** *(see Special Stitches)* in ch sp of next shell**, sc in next fpdc, rep from * around, ending last rep at **, join in beg sc. Fasten off.

SLEEVES

Rnd 1: Join lavender in center ch of ch-7 at armhole, **ch 2** *(see Pattern Notes)*, hdc in same ch, hdc in each of next 3 chs, 2 hdc in end of row 5, 2 hdc in each of next 12 sk sts, 2 hdc in end of row 5, hdc in each of last 3 chs, join in beg hdc. *(35 hdc)*

Rnds 2 & 3: Ch 2, hdc in first st and in each st around, join in beg hdc.

Rnd 4: Ch 1, **sc dec** *(see Stitch Guide)* in first 2 sts, [sc dec in next 2 sts] around, ending with sc in last st, join in beg sc. Fasten off. *(18 sc)*

EDGING

Working in **front lps** *(see Stitch Guide)*, join white in any st, ch 3, [sl st in next st, ch 3] around, join in beg sl st. Fasten off.

Rep in rem armhole.

BLOOMERS

Rnd 1: With lavender, ch 36, being careful not to twist ch, sl st in first ch to form ring, ch 2, hdc in first ch and in each ch around, join in beg hdc. *(36 hdc)*

Rnds 2–6: Ch 2, hdc in first st and in each st around, join in beg hdc.

FIRST LEG

Rnd 1: Ch 3, sk first 18 sts, sl st in next st, ch 2, hdc in same st and in each of next 17 hdc, hdc in each ch of beg ch-3, join in beg hdc. *(21 hdc)*

Rnd 2: Ch 2, hdc in first st and in each st around, join in beg hdc.

Rnd 3: Working in front lps, ch 1, sc in first st, ch 2, [sc in next st, ch 2] around, join in beg sc. Fasten off.

2ND LEG

Rnd 1: Join lavender in first st on rnd 6, ch 2, hdc in same st and in each of next 17 sts, hdc in each of next 3 chs, join in beg hdc. *(21 hdc)*

Rnds 2 & 3: Rep rnds 2 and 3 of First Leg.

HAT

Rnd 1: With white, ch 2, 6 sc in 2nd ch from hook, join in beg sc. *(6 sc)*

Rnd 2: Ch 2, 2 hdc in first st and in each st around, join in beg hdc. *(12 hdc)*

Rnd 3: Ch 2, 2 hdc in first st, hdc in next st, [2 hdc in next st, hdc in next st] around, join in beg hdc. *(18 hdc)*

Rnd 4: Ch 2, 2 hdc in first st, hdc in each of next 2 sts, [2 hdc in next st, hdc in each of next 2 sts] around, join in beg hdc. *(24 hdc)*

Rnd 5: Ch 2, 2 hdc in first st, hdc in each of next 3 sts, [2 hdc in next st, hdc in each of next 3 sts] around, join in beg hdc. *(30 hdc)*

Rnd 6: Ch 2, 2 hdc in first st, hdc in each of next 4 sts, [2 hdc in next st, hdc in each of next 4 sts] around, join in beg hdc. *(36 hdc)*

Rnd 7: Ch 2, 2 hdc in first st, hdc in each of next 5 sts, [2 hdc in next st, hdc in each of next 5 sts] around, join in beg hdc. *(42 hdc)*

Rnd 8: Ch 2, 2 hdc in first st, hdc in each of next 6 sts, [2 hdc in next st, hdc in each of next 6 sts] around, join in beg hdc. *(48 hdc)*

Rnd 9: Ch 2, 2 hdc in first st, hdc in each of next 7 sts, [2 hdc in next st, hdc in each of next 7 sts] around, join in beg hdc. *(54 hdc)*

Rnd 10: Ch 2, hdc in first st and in each st around, join in beg hdc.

Rnd 11: Ch 1, sc dec in first 2 sts, sc in next st, [sc dec in next 2 sts, sc in next st] around, join in beg sc. *(36 sc)*

Rnds 12–14: Ch 1, sc in each st around, join in beg sc. At end of last rnd, fasten off.

EDGING

Join lavender in any st, ch 3, [sl st in next st, ch 3] around, join in beg sl st. Fasten off.

BOOTIE

MAKE 2.

Rnd 1: Beg at sole, with lavender, ch 8, 2 sc in 2nd ch from hook, sc in each of next 4 chs, hdc in next ch, 4 hdc in last ch, working on opposite side of ch, hdc in next ch, sc in each of next 4 chs, 2 sc in last ch, join in beg sc. *(18 sts)*

Rnd 2: Ch 1, 2 sc in first st, sc in each of next 5 sts, hdc in next st, 2 hdc in each of next 4 sts, hdc in next st, sc in each of next 5 sts, 2 sc in last st, join in **back lp** *(see Stitch Guide)* of beg sc. *(24 sts)*

Rnd 3: Working in back lps, ch 1, sc in each st around, join in both lps of beg sc.

Rnd 4: Ch 1, sc in each st around, join in beg sc.

Rnd 5: Ch 1, sc each of first 8 sts, [sc dec in next 2 sts] 4 times, sc in each of last 8 sts, join in beg sc. Fasten off. *(20 sc)*

SOCK

Rnd 6: Working in back lps, join white with sc in first st, sc in each of next 8 sts, sc dec in next 2 sts, sc in each of last 9 sts, join in beg sc. *(19 sc)*

Rnd 7: Ch 1, sc in each of first 7 sts, [sc dec in next 2 sts] 3 times, sc in each of last 6 sts, join in beg sc. *(16 sc)*

Rnd 8: Ch 1, sc in each st around, join in back lp of beg sc.

Rnd 9: Working in back lps, ch 3, dc in each st around, join in 3rd ch of beg ch-3. Fasten off.

STRAP

Working in rem lps of rnd 5, join lavender with sc in first st, sc in each of next 5 sts, ch 8, sk next 8 sts, sc in each of last 6 sts, join in beg sc. Fasten off. ■

Ladybug Sundress & Jacket

SKILL LEVEL

INTERMEDIATE

FINISHED SIZE

Fits 5-inch baby doll

MATERIALS

- Size 10 crochet cotton:
  200 yds red
  100 yds black
  25 yds white
- Size 6/1.80mm steel crochet hook or size needed to obtain gauge
- Tapestry needle
- Sewing needle
- White sewing thread
- Small lady bug buttons: 2
- Small snap

GAUGE

9 sc = 1 inch; 8 sc rows = 1 inch
15 hdc = 2 inches; 7 hdc rows = 1 inch

PATTERN NOTES

Chain-2 at beginning of row or round does not count as first half double crochet unless otherwise stated.

Chain-3 at beginning of row or round counts as first double crochet unless otherwise stated.

Join with slip stitch as indicated unless otherwise stated.

INSTRUCTIONS

SUNDRESS

Row 1: Beg at neck, with red, ch 29, 2 sc in 2nd ch from hook and in each ch across, turn. *(56 sc)*

Row 2: Ch 1, sc in each of first 8 sts, ch 6, sk next 12 sts *(armhole)*, sc in each of next 16 sts, ch 6, sk next 12 sts *(armhole)*, sc in each of last 8 sts, turn.

Row 3: Ch 1, sc in each st and in each ch across, turn. *(44 sc)*

Rows 4–6: Ch 1, sc in each st across, turn.

Row 7: **Ch 3** *(see Pattern Notes)*, dc in same st, 2 dc in each st across, turn. *(88 dc)*

Rnd 8: Now working in rnds, ch 3, dc in each st around, **join** *(see Pattern Notes)* in 3rd ch of beg ch-3.

Rnds 9–11: Ch 3, dc in each st around, join in 3rd ch of beg ch-3.

EDGING

Rnd 12: Working in **front lps** *(see Stitch Guide)*, ch 1, sc in first st, ch 10, sc in same st, [ch 10, (sc, ch 10, sc) in next st] around, ch 10, join in both lps of beg sc. Fasten off.

JACKET

Row 1: With black, ch 30, 2 hdc in 3rd ch from hook and in each ch across, turn. *(56 hdc)*

Row 2: **Ch 2** *(see Pattern Notes)*, hdc in first st and in each of next 7 sts, ch 7, sk next 12 sts *(armhole)*, hdc in each of next 16 sts, ch 7, sk next 12 sts *(armhole)*, hdc in each of next 8 sts, turn.

Row 3: Ch 2, sk first st, hdc in each st and in each ch across with **hdc dec** *(see Stitch Guide)* in last 2 sts, turn. *(44 hdc)*

Row 4: Ch 2, sk first st, hdc in each st across with hdc dec in last 2 sts, turn. *(42 hdc)*

EDGING

Working around outer edge and in ends of rows, ch 1, (sc, ch 5, sc) in first st, ch 5, [(sc, ch 5, sc) in next st, ch 5] across with sc in last st, working in ends of rows, sc in each row across to neck, working in starting ch on opposite side of row 1, 2 sc in first ch, ch 1, [sc in next ch, ch 1] across, 2 sc in last ch, working in ends of rows, sc in end of first row, ch 3 *(button lp)*, sc in end of each row across, join in beg sc. Fasten off.

SLEEVES

Rnd 1: Join black in center ch at armhole, ch 2, hdc in same ch, hdc in each of next 3 chs, hdc in end of row 2, hdc in each of next 12 sk sts, hdc in end of row 2, hdc in each ch around, join in beg hdc. *(21 hdc)*

Rnds 2–6: Ch 2, hdc in first st and in each st around, join in beg hdc.

Rnd 7: Ch 1, **sc dec** *(see Stitch Guide)* in first 2 sts, sc in next st, [sc dec in next 2 sts, sc in next st] around, join in beg sc.

Rnd 8: Ch 1, (sc, ch 3, sc) in first st, ch 3, [(sc, ch 3, sc) in next st, ch 3] around, join in beg sc. Fasten off.

Rep in rem armhole.

Sew button opposite buttonhole.

PANTIES

FRONT

Row 1: With red, ch 4, sc in 2nd ch from hook and in each ch across, turn. *(3 sc)*

Row 2 (RS): Ch 1, sc in each st across, turn.

Rows 3–10: Ch 1, 2 sc in first st, sc in each st across to last st, 2 sc in last st, turn. At end of last row, fasten off. *(19 sc at end of last row)*

BACK

Row 1: Working in starting ch on opposite side of row 1 on Front, with WS facing, join red with sc in first ch, sc in each ch across, turn. *(3 sc)*

Row 2 (RS): Ch 1, sc in each st across, turn.

Rows 3–11: Ch 1, 2 sc in first st, sc in each st across to last st, 2 sc in last st, turn. *(21 sc at end of last row)*

Rnd 12: Joining Front and Back tog, ch 1, 2 sc in first st, sc in each st across with 2 sc in last st, sc in first st on Front, sc in each st across, join in beg sc. Fasten off.

EDGING

Join black with sc in beg ch, evenly sp 23 sc around leg opening, join in beg sc. Fasten off. *(24 sc)*

Rep on rem leg opening.

HEADBAND

Rnd 1: With white, ch 35, make sure it fits around head, being careful not to twist ch, sl st in first ch to form ring, ch 1, sc in each ch around, join in beg sc.

Rnd 2: Ch 1, sc in each st around, join in beg sc. Fasten off.

EDGING

Join black in first st, ch 3, [sl st in next st, ch 3] around, join in beg sl st. Fasten off.

Working in starting ch on opposite side of rnd 1, join black in first ch, ch 3, [sl st in next ch, ch 3] around, join in beg sl st. Fasten off.

Sew rem button to Headband as shown in photo.

BOOTIE

MAKE 2.

Rnd 1: Beg at sole, with black, ch 8, 2 sc in 2nd ch from hook, sc in each of next 4 chs, hdc in next ch, 4 hdc in last ch, working on opposite side of ch, hdc in next ch, sc in each of next 4 chs, 2 sc in last ch, join in beg sc. *(18 sts)*

Rnd 2: Ch 1, 2 sc in first st, sc in each of next 5 sts, hdc in next st, 2 hdc in each of next 4 sts, hdc in next st, sc in each of next 5 sts, 2 sc in last st, join in **back lp** *(see Stitch Guide)* of beg sc. *(24 sts)*

Rnd 3: Working in back lps, ch 1, sc in each st around, join in both lps of beg sc.

Rnd 4: Ch 1, sc in each st around, join in beg sc.

Rnd 5: Ch 1, sc each of first 8 sts, [sc dec in next 2 sts] 4 times, sc in each of last 8 sts, join in beg sc. Fasten off. *(20 sc)*

SOCK

Rnd 6: Working in back lps, join white with sc in first st, sc in each of next 8 sts, sc dec in next 2 sts, sc in each of last 9 sts, join in beg sc. *(19 sc)*

Rnd 7: Ch 1, sc in each of first 7 sts, [sc dec in next 2 sts] 3 times, sc in each of last 6 sts, join in beg sc. *(16 sc)*

Rnd 8: Ch 1, sc in each st around, join in back lp of beg sc.

Rnd 9: Working in back lps, ch 3, dc in each st around, join in 3rd ch of beg ch-3. Fasten off.

STRAP

Working in rem lps of rnd 5, join black in first st, sc in each of next 5 sts, ch 8, sk next 8 sts, sc in each of last 6 sts, join in beg sc. Fasten off. ■

Take Me To The Park

SKILL LEVEL

INTERMEDIATE

FINISHED SIZE

Fits 5-inch baby doll

MATERIALS

- Size 10 crochet cotton:
  150 yds white
  100 yds navy
- Sizes 10/1.15mm and 6/1.80mm steel crochet hooks or size needed to obtain gauge
- Tapestry needle
- Sewing needle
- White sewing thread
- Tiny buttons: 2
- Small snap
- Stitch marker

GAUGE

9 sc = 1 inch; 8 sc rows = 1 inch
15 hdc= 2 inches; 7 hdc rows = 1 inch

PATTERN NOTES

Use size 6 crochet hook unless otherwise stated.

Chain-2 at beginning of row or round does not count as first half double crochet unless otherwise stated.

Join with slip stitch as indicated unless otherwise stated.

INSTRUCTIONS

ONESIE

T-SHIRT FRONT

Row 1: Beg at bottom, with white and **size 6 hook** *(see Pattern Notes)*, ch 4, sc in 2nd ch from hook and in each ch across, turn. *(3 sc)*

Row 2 (RS): Ch 1, sc in each st across, turn.

Rows 3–11: Ch 1, 2 sc in first st, sc in each st across with 2 sc in last st, turn. At end of last row, fasten off. *(21 sc at end of last row)*

T-SHIRT BACK

Row 1: With RS facing, working in starting ch on opposite side of row 1 on T-Shirt Front, join white with sc in first ch, sc in each ch across, turn. *(3 sc)*

Rows 2–11: Ch 1, 2 sc in first st, sc in each st across with 2 sc in last st, turn. **At end of last row, do not turn or fasten off.** *(21 sc at end of last row)*

Rnd 12: Now working in rnds, ch 1, 2 sc in first st, sc in each st across with 2 sc in last st, sc in first st on T-Shirt Front, sc in each st across, **join** *(see Pattern Notes)* in beg sc. *(44 sc)*

Rnd 13: Ch 2 *(see Pattern Notes)*, hdc in first st and in each st around, join in beg hdc. Fasten off.

T-SHIRT TOP

Row 1: Now working in rows, with RS facing, sk first 12 sts, join white in next st, ch 2, hdc in first st and each st across, including the first 12 sk sts, turn, **do not join**. *(44 sc)*

Row 2: Ch 2, hdc in first st and in each st across, turn.

ARMHOLE SHAPING

Row 3: Ch 2, hdc in first st and in each of next 9 sts, ch 10, sk next 5 sts *(armhole)*, hdc in each of next 14 sts, ch 10, sk next 5 sts *(armhole)*, hdc in each of last 10 sts, turn. *(34 hdc)*

Row 4: Ch 2, hdc in first st and in each st and ch across, turn. *(54 hdc)*

Row 5: Ch 1, sc in each of first 3 sts, **sc dec** *(see Stitch Guide)* in next 2 sts, [sc in each of next 2 sts, sc dec in next 2 sts] across, ending with 2 sc in last st, turn. *(42 sc)*

Row 6: Ch 1, sc in each of first 2 sts, sc dec in next 2 sts, [sc in next st, sc dec in next 2 sts] across, ending with sc in each of last 2 sts. Fasten off. *(29 sc)*

SLEEVE

Rnd 1: Join white in center sk st at armhole, ch 2, hdc in same st, hdc in each of next 2 sts, **hdc dec** *(see Stitch Guide)* in end of row 3 and first ch of ch-10 on row 3, hdc in each of next 8 chs, hdc dec in last ch and end of row 3, hdc in each of last 2 sk sts, join in beg hdc. *(15 hdc)*

Rnds 2 & 3: Ch 2, hdc in first st and in each st around, join in beg hdc. At end of last rnd, fasten off.

Rep on rem armhole.

LEG EDGING

Join white with sc in end of row 1 on T-Shirt Back, evenly sp 23 sc around leg opening, join in beg sc. Fasten off. *(24 sc)*

Rep on opposite leg opening.

Sew snap at top edge of back opening.

OVERALLS

FRONT BIB

Row 1 (RS): With navy, ch 10, hdc in 3rd ch from hook and in each ch across, turn. *(8 hdc)*

Rows 2–5: Ch 2, hdc in first st and in each st across, turn. At end of last row, ch 28, being careful not to twist ch, join in beg hdc.

WAIST

Rnd 6: Now working in rnds, ch 2, hdc in first st and in each st and ch around, join in beg hdc. *(36 hdc)*

Rnds 7–11: Ch 2, hdc in each st around, join in beg hdc.

FIRST LEG OPENING

Rnd 1: Sl st in each of next 8 sts, place marker in last st, ch 3, sk next 17 sts, sl st in next st, ch 2, hdc in same st and in each of next 17 sts, including the beg 8 sl sts, hdc in each of next 3 chs, join in beg hdc. *(21 hdc)*

Rnds 2–5: Ch 2, hdc in first st and in each st around, join in beg hdc. At end of last rnd, fasten off.

2ND LEG OPENING

Rnd 1: With RS facing and front of Bib facing down, join in marked st, ch 2, hdc in same st and in each of next 17 sts, hdc in each of next 3 chs, join in beg hdc. *(21 hdc)*

Rnds 2–5: Ch 2, hdc in first st and in each st around, join in beg hdc. At end of last rnd, fasten off.

FIRST STRAP

Row 1: With RS facing and Overalls RS up, counting from right edge of Bib, working on opposite side of ch at Waist, count 12 chs to right, join navy in next ch, ch 2, hdc in each of next 2 sts, leaving rem chs unworked, turn. *(1 ch-2, 2 hdc)*

Rows 2–13: Ch 2, hdc in same st and in next st, turn. *(2 hdc)*

Try on doll to make sure Strap is long enough. You can add or dec rows as necessary.

Buttonhole row: Ch 3 *(counts as first dc)*, dc in next st, turn.

Last row: Ch 1, sc in each of first 2 sts. Fasten off.

2ND STRAP

Row 1: With RS facing, sk next 5 sts to right of where First Strap was joined on Waist, join navy in next st, ch 2, hdc in same st, hdc dec in next 2 sts, leaving rem sts unworked, turn.

Rows 2–13: Ch 2, hdc in same st and in next st, turn. *(2 hdc)*

Try on doll to make sure Strap is long enough. You can add or dec rows as necessary.

Buttonhole row: Ch 3 *(counts as first dc)*, dc in next st, turn.

Last row: Ch 1, sc in each of first 2 sts. Fasten off.

EDGING

Join navy with sc in any ch on opposite side of ch at Waist, sc in each ch around with evenly sp sc in ends of rows of Bib and Straps, join in first sc. Fasten off.

Sew buttons to front of Bib at top corners as shown in photo.

HIGH TOP BOOTIES

MAKE 2.

Rnd 1 (RS): Beg at sole, with navy, ch 8, 2 sc in 2nd ch from hook, sc in each of next 4 chs, hdc in next ch, 4 hdc in last ch, working on opposite side of ch, hdc in next ch, sc in each of next 4 chs, 2 sc in last ch, join in beg sc. *(18 sts)*

Rnd 2: Ch 1, 2 sc in first st, sc in each of next 5 sts, hdc in next st, 2 hdc in each of next 4 sts, hdc in next st, sc in each of next 5 sts, 2 sc in last st, join in **back lp** *(see Stitch Guide)* of beg sc. Fasten off. *(24 sts)*

Rnd 3: Working in back lps, join white in first st, sc in each st around, join in both lps of beg sc.

Rnd 4: Ch 1, sc in each st around, join in beg sc.

Rnd 5: Ch 1, sc in each of first 8 sts, [sc dec in next 2 sts] 4 times, sc in each of last 8 sts, join in beg sc. *(20 sc)*

Rnd 6: Ch 1, sc in each st around, join in beg sc.

Rnd 7: Ch 1, sc in each of first 6 sts, [sc dec in next 2 sts] 4 times, sc in each of last 6 sts, join in beg sc. *(16 sc)*

Rnd 8: Ch 1, sc in each st around, join in beg sc. Fasten off.

BASEBALL HAT

Rnd 1: With white, ch 2, 6 sc in 2nd ch from hook, join in beg sc. *(6 sc)*

Rnd 2: Ch 2, 2 hdc in first st and in each st around, join in beg hdc. *(12 hdc)*

Rnd 3: Ch 2, 2 hdc in first st, hdc in next st, [2 hdc in next st, hdc in next st] around, join in beg hdc. *(18 hdc)*

Rnd 4: Ch 2, 2 hdc in first st, hdc in each of next 2 sts, [2 hdc in next st, 2 hdc in each of next 2 sts] around, join in beg hdc. *(24 hdc)*

Rnd 5: Ch 2, 2 hdc in first st, hdc in each of next 3 sts, [2 hdc in next st, 2 hdc in each of next 3 sts] around, join in beg hdc. *(30 hdc)*

Rnds 6 & 7: Ch 2, hdc in first st and in each st around, join in beg hdc.

Rnd 8: Ch 2, 2 hdc in first st, hdc in each of next 5 sts, [2 hdc in next st, 2 hdc in each of next 5 sts] around, join in beg hdc. *(35 hdc)*

Rnds 9 & 10: Ch 2, hdc in first st and in each st around, join in beg hdc. At end of last rnd, fasten off.

STRIPES

Using **straight stitch** *(see Fig. 1)*, with blue, embroider stripes starting at every 5th st on rnd 10 up to center of rnd 1 for a total of 7 stripes as shown in photo.

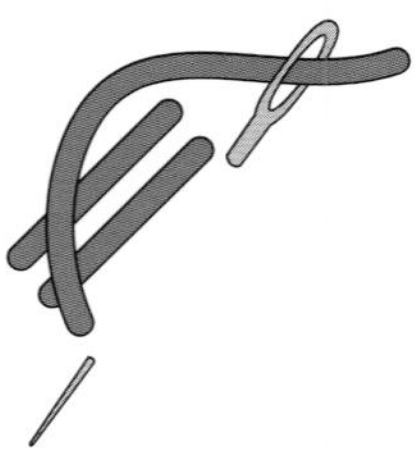

Fig. 1
Straight Stitch

BRIM & BILL

Working in back lps, join navy in any st on rnd 10, sc in next st, hdc in next st, 2 dc in each of next 6 sts, hdc in next st, sc in next st, sl st in each of next 2 sts, working in both lps, ch 1, sc in next st, mark this st, sc in each st around, working in sts at beg of this rnd, sc in each st across to marker, join in marked sc. Fasten off.

CIRCLE

With navy and size 10 hook, ch 2, 6 sc in 2nd ch from hook, join in beg sc. Leaving long end, fasten off.

With long end, sew Circle to center top of Hat as shown in photo. ■

TOLL-FREE ORDER LINE or to request a free catalog (800) LV-ANNIE (800) 582-6643
Customer Service (800) AT-ANNIE (800) 282-6643, **Fax** (800) 882-6643
Visit AnniesAttic.com

ISBN: 978-1-59635-248-3

Printed in USA

2 3 4 5 6 7 8 9

Stitch Guide

For more complete information, visit **FreePatterns.com**

ABBREVIATIONS

beg	begin/begins/beginning
bpdc	back post double crochet
bpsc	back post single crochet
bptr	back post treble crochet
CC	contrasting color
ch(s)	chain(s)
ch-	refers to chain or space previously made (e.g., ch-1 space)
ch sp(s)	chain space(s)
cl(s)	cluster(s)
cm	centimeter(s)
dc	double crochet (singular/plural)
dc dec	double crochet 2 or more stitches together, as indicated
dec	decrease/decreases/decreasing
dtr	double treble crochet
ext	extended
fpdc	front post double crochet
fpsc	front post single crochet
fptr	front post treble crochet
g	gram(s)
hdc	half double crochet
hdc dec	half double crochet 2 or more stitches together, as indicated
inc	increase/increases/increasing
lp(s)	loop(s)
MC	main color
mm	millimeter(s)
oz	ounce(s)
pc	popcorn(s)
rem	remain/remains/remaining
rep(s)	repeat(s)
rnd(s)	round(s)
RS	right side
sc	single crochet (singular/plural)
sc dec	single crochet 2 or more stitches together, as indicated
sk	skip/skipped/skipping
sl st(s)	slip stitch(es)
sp(s)	space(s)/spaced
st(s)	stitch(es)
tog	together
tr	treble crochet
trtr	triple treble
WS	wrong side
yd(s)	yard(s)
yo	yarn over

Chain—ch: Yo, pull through lp on hook.

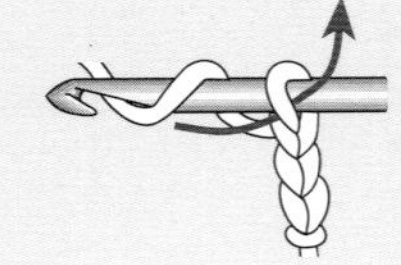

Slip stitch—sl st: Insert hook in st, pull through both lps on hook.

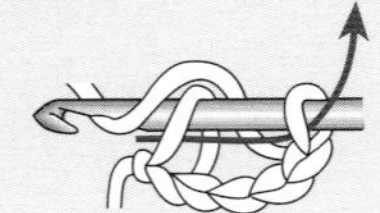

Single crochet—sc: Insert hook in st, yo, pull through st, yo, pull through both lps on hook.

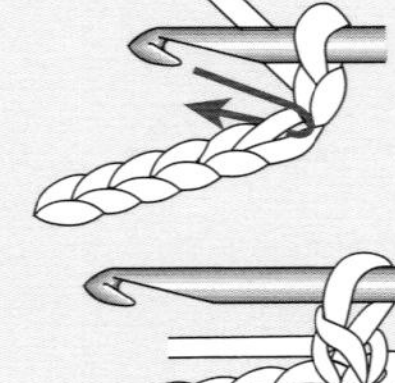

Front post stitch—fp:
Back post stitch—bp: When working post st, insert hook from right to left around post st on previous row.

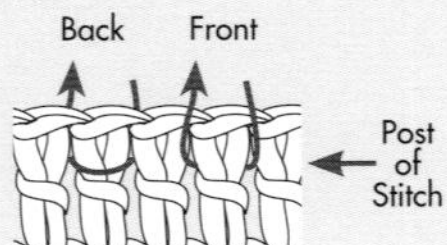

Front loop—front lp
Back loop—back lp

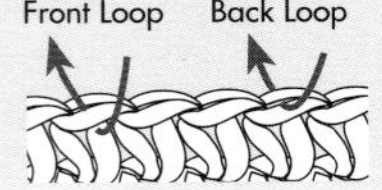

Half double crochet—hdc: Yo, insert hook in st, yo, pull through st, yo, pull through all 3 lps on hook.

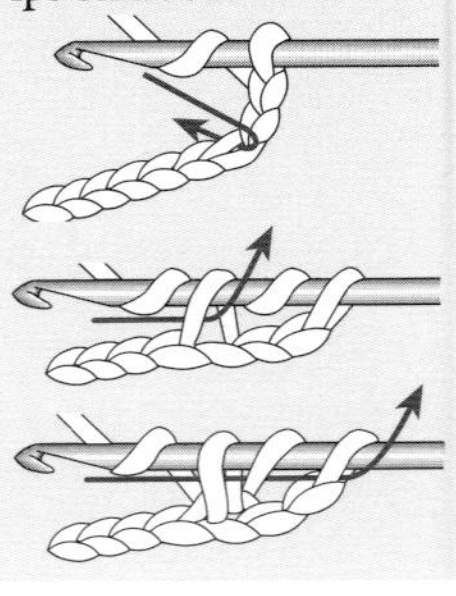

Double crochet—dc: Yo, insert hook in st, yo, pull through st, [yo, pull through 2 lps] twice.

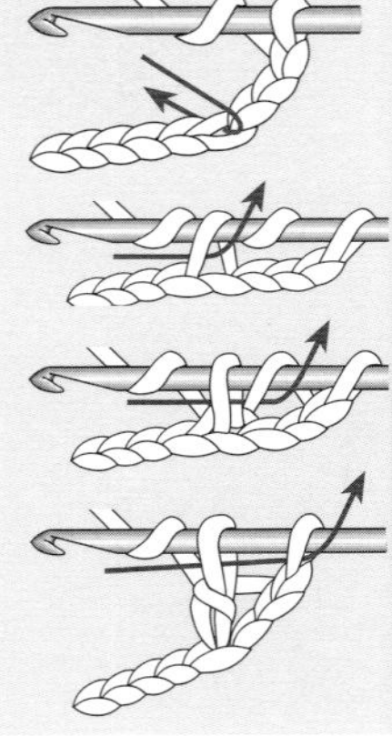

Change colors: Drop first color; with 2nd color, pull through last 2 lps of st.

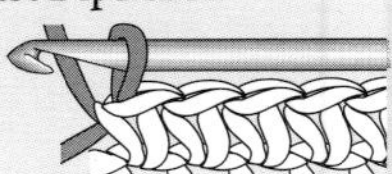

Treble crochet—tr: Yo twice, insert hook in st, yo, pull through st, [yo, pull through 2 lps] 3 times.

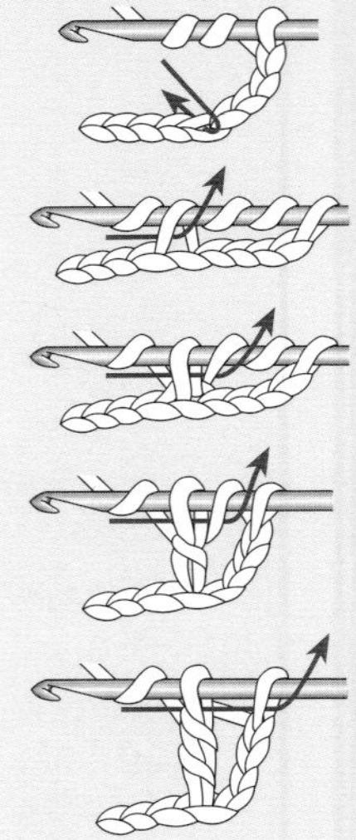

Double treble crochet—dtr: Yo 3 times, insert hook in st, yo, pull through st, [yo, pull through 2 lps] 4 times.

Single crochet decrease (sc dec): (Insert hook, yo, draw lp through) in each of the sts indicated, yo, draw through all lps on hook.

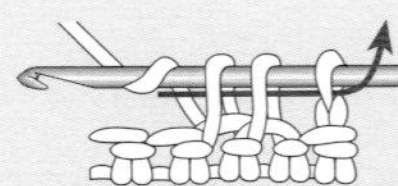

Example of 2-sc dec

Half double crochet decrease (hdc dec): (Yo, insert hook, yo, draw lp through) in each of the sts indicated, yo, draw through all lps on hook.

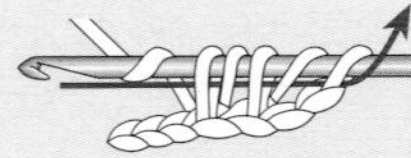

Example of 2-hdc dec

Double crochet decrease (dc dec): (Yo, insert hook, yo, draw loop through, draw through 2 lps on hook) in each of the sts indicated, yo, draw through all lps on hook.

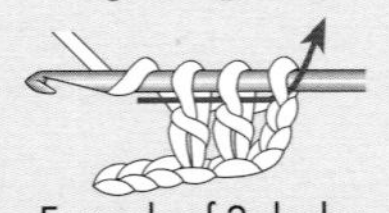

Example of 2-dc dec

Example of 2-tr dec

Treble crochet decrease (tr dec): Holding back last lp of each st, tr in each of the sts indicated, yo, pull through all lps on hook.

US		**UK**
sl st (slip stitch)	=	sc (single crochet)
sc (single crochet)	=	dc (double crochet)
hdc (half double crochet)	=	htr (half treble crochet)
dc (double crochet)	=	tr (treble crochet)
tr (treble crochet)	=	dtr (double treble crochet)
dtr (double treble crochet)	=	ttr (triple treble crochet)
skip	=	miss